Plaster techniques

Plaster techniques

van Dobbenburgh Amsterdam/Kidderminster

Original titel. Gips technieken
Editor: Lies de Jonge
Translation from the Dutch
The Old Rectory, Pyworthy,
Holsworthy, Devon. Ex 22 6LA, England

English Edition distributed by
Ruskin Book services Ltd.
15 Comberton Hill, Kidderminster
Worcestershire DY 10 1QG U.K.
Telephone 0562 515151 and 68014
Telex RBS 335672
Printed in Spain by I.G. Domingo, S.A. San Joan Despí

ISBN 9-06-577033-x

Contents

Plaster is a very versatile material

Great artists have always been prepared to admit that their ideas would be far less easy to realize without the help of plaster of Paris. They are not alone in this, and this book shows how amateurs can also profit from this exceptionally useful and easy-to-work material. The reader will discover the many uses of plaster in step-by-step descriptions: modelling, carving, making moulds, reliefs and sculptures – an almost inexhaustible list of possibilities.

Plaster is extremely easy to use, but it also has the peculiar quality of penetrating every nook and cranny of a shape, and of drying very quickly.

Nevertheless, it is not one of the 'noble' materials that have been used for centuries to create great works of art; the material is too fragile and impermanent. It has always been used as an aid in two important branches of the arts: sculpture and ceramics, and for these two art forms it has always had the same meaning.

It forms the basis for the final work of art.

In addition, plaster has proved an essential aid in industrial design, particularly in the ceramic industry. Two aspects of this cannot be undervalued: an extremely strong design and the possibility of reproducing this quickly, an infinite number of times.

Plaster is the perfect material for this. It is used to create the design, and this in turn forms the basis of the mould. In this way the three most important subjects of the book are all presented – casting in plaster, making the model and constructing the moulds, which may consist of one or more parts. The medium is introduced step by step and the use of tools is described so that the reader can learn to master the techniques required.

Because of the large variety of techniques described with accompanying photographs, this book serves as a manual for people who have never worked with plaster before, as well as for those who wish to improve their skill in the medium.

Things you need to know about plaster of Paris
Plaster of Paris comes as a powder and goes hard when water is added. There are many different sorts of plaster, but as only two are used in this book, they are the only two mentioned here.

1. Modelling plaster: this is relatively cheap and is more suitable for fairly coarse work such as experimenting with casting moulds, studies in form, and for sculpture or modelling.
2. Casting plaster: this material has a finer structure, goes hard faster and is mainly used for casting. It is a more expensive plaster, but the results are also better. As you usually use a large quantity of plaster to cast figures, it may work out more economical to buy in bulk. However, remember that it will not keep for very long. It should always be stored in a sealed container or bucket. In fact, this applies to any sort of plaster. The powder can be purchased in shops selling artists' materials or specialists in products for pottery.

A fast setting material
As mentioned above, plaster has to be mixed with water to go hard. The correct mixing technique depends on having the correct proportions and on experience.
Before you start, remember that it is important to always read the instructions on the labels, and do not forget that the plaster goes hard very fast. For this reason you must work quickly and effectively.

The correct order
Always mix the plaster in a clean plastic container, a tray or a bucket, and use cold tap water. Use the proportion 1 part water to $1^{1}/_{2}$ to 2 parts plaster.
To measure the quantities use a dry plastic measuring beaker and be as accurate as possible. In this way you prevent the plaster going hard too quickly or too slowly – or even failing to go hard at all.
The best quality is achieved by measuring the quantities as accurately as possible. Always start with the water and add the plaster, never the other way round.
Sprinkle the plaster evenly into the water with your hand until there is a mound of plaster on the surface of the water. Leave this to stand for about a minute and then stir in with the hand. In this way any lumps in the mixture can easily be rubbed fine.
It is absolutely essential for good plaster work that there are no lumps or air bubbles in the plaster mix whatsoever. Air bubbles cause ugly holes in your plaster work which can be removed, but it is better to prevent them in the first place.
To prevent air bubbles occuring, you should tap on the side a few times at the end of the process. All the air bubbles in the plaster will come up as a result of the vibrations, and they can then be scooped off the surface with the hand. This should not be left too long as the plaster soon starts to go hard.
Gauging the correct consistency is a question of experience, but at first it is best to assume that the plaster mixture should have roughly the consistency of yoghurt when it has been thoroughly mixed.

Working quickly and effectively
When all the lumps and any airbubbles in the plaster have been removed, it is time to use the plaster.
It should be used quickly and effectively, for after about 6 to 8 minutes the plaster is barely liquid, and after about 15 minutes it can no longer be spread.
This is followed by the hardening of the plaster, which releases heat.
From this point onwards you cannot really alter your work until the next stage, which usually takes another $1^{1}/_{2}$ to 2 hours. After the casting process the edges or can be removed, and the surfaces and sides can be smoothed out.

Separating agents
Plaster is a material which easily adheres to any other material, although this is not usually the intention.
There are a number of ways of preventing the plaster from sticking to things. In some cases it may be necessary to use two agents.
1. A diluted soap solution makes a very suitable separating agent. This is made by dissolving liquid (green) soap or a bar of soap in hot water and leaving this to stand for about a day. The proportions are usually one part soap to two parts water.
2. Oil or vaseline can also be used as a separating agent. Use any type of household oil, such as salad oil.
3. Another possible separating agent is a solution of shellac in methylated spirits. To make this, fill a bottle with finely rubbed shellac, which you can buy from a chemist. Heat this up au bain marie without the cork on the bottle. Shake thoroughly. When the solution has cooled down it is ready for use.

Special tools and materials

Plaster of Paris is a material which can be used for many different purposes and which can also be worked in many different ways. One advantage of this material is that the tools required do not have to be expensive.
The more you use the material, the more specialised the tools you will start to acquire. However, to start with you can simply use the tools you will find at home. These can easily be used to make some beautiful works.

The tools shown in the photograph below are specifically for working with plaster of Paris, but it is certainly not necessary to acquire all of them straightaway. Once the plaster has hardened it can be worked in different ways. You can change the shape of the plaster, for example, by grinding it, or by using a chisel on it, rather like sculpture. For grinding or filing it you will need a rasp. These are actually very coarse files for wood which have small metal hooks. As these hooks are quite far apart, the material is easily removed. This is ideal for plaster. Another ideal tool is an old Surform (open blade). Instead of these tools you can use a fairly coarse file – for example, a block file. A disadvantage of this type of file is that it tends to get clogged up easily. You can avoid this problem by regularly cleaning it with a steel wire brush. This brush can also be used to clean graters and other tools. Plaster is an ideal tool for making reliefs. For these you use a wooden hammer, chisels and a gouge. Chisels are flat, while gouges have a semi-circular or triangular side. It is best to use a chisel for cutting off bits of plaster and smoothing the surface, while the gouge is used to make grooves and depressions of various depths. It is always worth having a look in your tool box before buying any new tools. When you are working with plaster it is essential for the tools to be free of rust.
Learning to use tools through practice
It is also possible to saw through plaster. For this it is best to use a hacksaw with a detachable blade.
Provided that it has not gone completely hard, which takes about three days, the plaster can easily be scraped or cut. To do

this, use a scraper and a sharp knife. The former is easily made from a piece of tin or you can use an old metal rule for this purpose. Here we give only a few examples, but experience will soon show you that virtually any tool can be replaced simply.
If you do decide to buy new tools, you need only start with the equipment shown in the photograph. We also include a short list of all the tools which you will meet as you work your way through the book.

1. Graters and modelling tools
2. Turning tools
3. Saw blades
4. Pieces of tin (0.8 mm) broad elastic, scrapers
5. Covers and other modelling tools
6. Wooden mallet
7. Separating and dissolving agents: soap and oil. (These ensure that the plaster can easily be removed from the mould.)
8. Bowls made of plastic and a sponge.

Making a flat tile

In order to get to know this material we have chosen a straightforward project – casting a flat plate or tile. The exercises following this one show you what you can do with this sort of plate. Before starting on the exercises on the following pages, here is some general information and practical tips.

As mentioned above, there are two different types of plaster to use. To make a flat tile it is advisable to use the finer modelling plaster. This does not take as long to set and goes slightly harder. Determining the correct quantity is always a bit of a gamble.

However, there is a way of working out the quantities you will roughly need. The method is described below.

A plaster plate or tile is always cast in a wooden frame. Imagine that this is 20 x 15 cm. and 5 cm. deep. Start by calculating the total content, i.e., length x width x depth. In this particular case this comes to 20 x 15 x 15 = 1500 cm^2.

This is 1½ litres of plaster.

To find out how much water you need, multiply the amount of plaster by about 0.5. 1500 x 0.5 = 750 cm^3.

This means that you should use roughly 3/4 litre of water and sprinkle the powdered plaster into this. The quantity of plaster is determined by its saturation point, which means in this case, that a layer of powder should lie on the surface of the water. When you have stirred in the powder and the lumps have dissolved, the plaster should be used as quickly as possible before it begins to set. Always work quickly and efficiently.

1

To make a flat tile you will need a wooden frame, a piece of plastic coated hardboard or a glass plate, a bowl of powdered plaster, oil, a large bowl, a stirrer and a brush.

2

The sides of the frame are hinged together. Remove the hinge pin from one of the hinges.

3

Place the frame on the plastic coated hardboard or glass plate and shut the open hinge with a nail that fits.

4

Place the frame on the board or glass and surround with clay to prevent the plaster from draining away.

5

Use a brush to spread oil over the entire base and over the inside of the frame.

6

Mix the plaster and water in the bowl. The mixture should not go lumpy.

7

When there is a pile of plaster on the water, stop adding plaster.

8

Remove any lumps by stirring the mixture thoroughly with the hand.

9
Spoon the liquid plaster into the corners of the frame.

10
Spread the thin layer of plaster evenly over the base with your hand.

11
The rest of the plaster is poured from the bowl straight into the frame up to the required depth.

12
The plaster should be left to set and cool down naturally (approximately 2 hours). Then smooth the surface with a piece of tin or a metal rule.

13
Carefully tap the sides of the frame a few times with a wooden mallet. The plaster tile should come free very easily.

14
The simple tile made in this way is now used in the following exercise to achieve decorative results.

Making and painting a plaster relief

Now that you are acquainted with the material, you are ready to try out one of the many possible techniques used with plaster of Paris. In this example you make a relief on a flat tile. You will need some practice with this technique. The step-by-step approach on the following pages helps to explain the process and clearly shows you what to do.

A relief is always made using an entirely dry plaster board. The motif in our example is quite arbitrary, and obviously you can choose any other pattern, provided that you always work in the same order, i.e., start by working on the large parts of the design and then concentrate on the details. It is advisable to practice cutting away smoothly at first, before embarking on this type of project.

Remember that you cannot cut away large lumps of plaster at one go, but that layers and bits must be removed a little at a time. You will need flat chisels and gouges.

The chisels are used to remove large flat areas, while the gouges are used to put in the details. To paint the plaster you can use either acrylic or tempera paints.

Neither type of paint should be diluted with water too much, as plaster is a very absorbent material. However, if the paint still does not adhere properly to the surface, a drop of liquid soap will usually do the trick.

If the paint is diluted too much, the white background will show through and this will not improve the final result.

The relief is accentuated by the strongly contrasting colours. As a result, the work looks more attractive and natural.

1

In addition to a plaster tile, you will need a number of chisels and gouges, white sketching paper, carbon paper, a felt tip pen and a pencil.

2

Draw the motif you have chosen on the sheet of paper with a felt tip pen.

3

Place the carbon paper between the plaster tile and the design and go over the design with a pencil.

4

The whole design should be clearly shown on the plaster tile. If necessary, fill in any lines that are missing or not clear.

5

Use a wide flat chisel to remove the plaster around the design.

6

To prevent damage to the ouline of the design, carefully remove layer by layer.

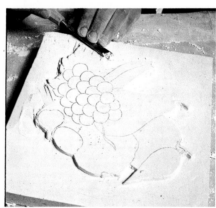

7

The design now seems to be lying on the plaster.

8

Use a chisel with a narrower end and semi-circular gouges to do the difficult shapes.

9 Separating the individual parts of the design is an exacting and painstaking process. For the finest detail it is advisable to use a knife.

10 The various parts are now at the stage where they can be finished off with various grades of sandpaper (medium fine/fine).

11 To paint the design you will need a number of paintbrushes (no. 4 and no. 6) and a few different coloured paints.

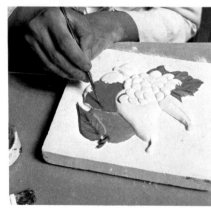

12 Use a brush (no. 6) to apply the paint. Make sure that the paint is not too diluted.

13 Use the same brush for the orange paint. Rinse the brush thoroughly in water.

14 A relief based on this sort of design with fruit looks best when bright contrasting colours are used.

15 Contrasting shades. The most vivid colours are kept for the middle of the design.

16 The colours are applied in such a way that the shapes and the difference in depth is emphasized. Make sure that your hand does not rest on an area where the paint is wet.

Plaster relief with birds of paradise

After the colourful still life described in the previous example, this is a project with a more subtle and detailed relief. The smaller finer detail means that you must use the chisel and gouge even more carefully and precisely than in the previous work.

Carving this exotic example is an extremely precise and painstaking project, but you will find that the beautiful end result is well worth the effort.

1 For this relief you will need paper, carbon paper, a pencil, a set of chisels and a plaster tile.

2 Draw the design onto a sheet of paper first.

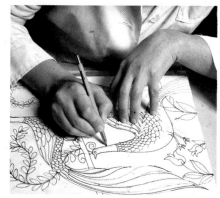

3 Transfer the design onto the plaster tile with carbon paper.

4 Go over any lines which are not clear with pencil to ensure that the design is absolutely complete.

5 Start by cutting away the plaster at the top where there is no drawing.

6 Continue with the part of the picture directly below this. Cut away the parts which should not be raised, but leave out the finer detail for the time being.

7 The outlines of the birds at the top are becoming clear.

8 When you have finished the main lines of the design, carefully start working on the detail.

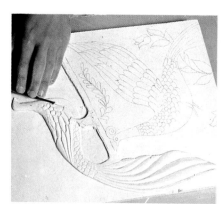

9

The feathers of the birds are also shown in relief. This extremely detailed work must be carried out completely accurately. For the finest detail use a gouge instead of a chisel.

10

When you have completed the top half of the design, continue with the bottom half in the same way.

11

Again the details are cut down extremely accurately with as much relief as possible.

12

The flower motif in the empty spaces is carefully carved out with a small triangular gouge.

13

The end result is a beautiful white relief. Obviously it is possible to paint this in beautifully exotic colours.

Plaster casting with a 'lost' mould

Why is plaster used so often for casting? This is simply because it guarantees an accurate and faithful reproduction like no other material can. Various methods of making plaster moulds are described in this chapter and the following chapters, from very basic, simple techniques to the professional techniques that are used. In order to cast the plaster you will always need a mould.

This photograph shows an accurate plaster cast of an original model made of clay. Both the clay model and the mould are lost when this method is used.

The mould can be made in a number of different ways. In the first place you will need a basic model, i.e., the original. There are two methods, the so-called 'lost' and 'not lost' methods. In the first case the mould is destroyed and only one cast is made. In the second case the mould is kept, so that you can make more than one identical reproduction. Ways of making the mould, whether it is used once or a number of times, are described later in the book.

Using colour as an aid
We have chosen a model of unfired plastic clay.
Another material could have been used instead, but for fast results, clay is easiest. You must remember that with this mould the material is disposed of. As the clay has not been fired, it can be thrown away once you have cast the plaster figure. The shape of the relief should be such that the plaster is not retained. This is known as a 'lost mould'. Obviously there are many possibilities with regard to this shape. However, in order to master the technique, start with a simple tile with relief, as in our example. The layer of plaster must not be cut away when it has set. This is an extremely accurate process, as the plaster cast must not be damaged. For this reason colour is added to simplify the process. The plaster is applied in two layers and a dye is added to the first, thin layer. The dye could be a powder dye (such as Dylon or Deka) dissolved in water

or a small amount of ecoline (watercolour).
This is mixed in with plaster when it is prepared. The first layer of plaster is then covered with a second layer of plain white plaster. When you are working you will realise that you must proceed very carefully once you reach the coloured layer, as this is the plaster cast.
A brief resumé of the process is given below by way of clarification.
1. The basic model is covered with two successive layers of plaster.
2. The clay is removed.
3. The resulting hollow is filled with liquid plaster.

4. The mould is smashed to reveal the plaster cast. Remember this important rule: control your curiosity to see the cast, and wait a little too long rather than too short.

Working with plaster
The previous chapters have shown that plaster is an easy material to work, with many different techniques.
You should become acquainted with the material by experimenting with it and adopting a step-by-step approach. Start with straightforward projects before attempting professional work. The following pages should be useful for this.

1
Make the model with clay that is still soft; this will be disposed of later on.

2
Finish off the relief with a modelling tool.

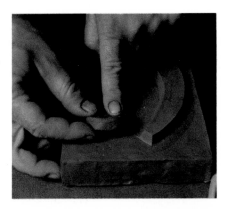

3
When the relief is completed it can be reproduced. Use a glass plate for the base.

4
For the first stage of the process you need some coils of clay, oil and a paintbrush.

5
Spread the oil onto the glass plate between the surround of clay coils and the model, using a paintbrush.

6
To make the 'lost' shape you will need powder paint, modelling plaster, water and a rod to stir the plaster.

7

Add a small amount of paint to the water.

8

Now add the plaster, making sure that there are no lumps.

9

Stir the mixture until it is an even colour and composition.

10

Spoon the coloured plaster evenly over the model.

11

The model should be covered with liquid plaster all over.

12

Prepare some more plaster, this time with water only.

13

When the plaster has been thoroughly stirred, spoon over the first layer of plaster. Together, the two layers will form a single mould.

14

When the mould is dry, smooth the surface with a modelling tool and scraper.

15
Remove the surround of coiled clay which prevented the plaster from spreading too far.

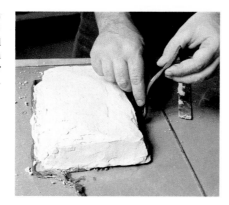

16
The mould is finished but the clay should not be removed for about two hours.

17
It is easy to remove the clay from the mould.

18
Work carefully so that you do not damage the inside of the mould.

19
The mould is empty and virtually clean.

20
Use a soft sponge dipped in diluted lye to clean the mould thoroughly.

21
Soap and oil are now added to the rest of the ingredients to ensure that the plaster can be easily removed from the mould at a later stage.

22
Dissolve the soap in water and spread over the mould with a brush.

23
Remove any soap that has not been absorbed and brush oil over the entire surface of the mould.

24
Prepare another lot of plaster, this time for the plaster cast.

25
Spread the plaster over the inside of the mould as shown in the photograph.

26
When the mould is full smooth the plaster with a modelling tool.

27
When the plaster has set, turn the mould and remove it bit by bit with a flat chisel and wooden mallet.

28
The coloured layer of plaster indicates that you are almost at the plaster cast.

29
At this stage work very carefully so as not to damage the plaster cast.

30
A perfect reproduction. Make sure that you thoroughly clean all the materials you have used.

A mould for a bowl or a dish made in one part

The first method of plaster casting was described in the preceding chapter. This section deals with moulds which can be used for making plaster casts one or more times. Thus the basic model can be reproduced as many times as you wish. You could make a whole series of bowls using this example.

Moulds are used in the ceramics industry on a large scale. In industry there is a need to use a model to make a number of castings, so it has to be possible to use the mould over and over again. This is known as casting a permanent mould. Depending on the basic model, this mould can consist of one or more parts; this depends on the shape of the model. In general one could say that the more complicated the basic shape is, the more parts are needed for the mould.

For small round shapes such as beakers, bowls and dishes, the mould can consist of just one part, provided that the shape is straight or with an outward slant at the top.

To make the mould you have to begin with a basic model. This model can be made of various materials and in many different ways. For example, if the model is round, it can be made on a potter's wheel or made by hand to the required size and shape. It is also possible to use an already existing figure, e.g., made of wood, earthenware or metal. You must make sure that you coat the figure with an oily substance such as vaseline or salad oil.

This will ensure that the plaster does not stick to the figure. The mould can be made directly round the basic model. In this example it will consist of a single part.

This plaster bowl has been cast from a mould consisting of one piece. It can be reproduced as often as desired using the step-by-step instructions given below.

1

Materials required: a bowl made of clay, earthenware or wood serves as a basic model; coils of clay, oil to use as a separating agent, and a glass plate.

2

Turn the bowl upside down on the glass plate and press the coil of clay down in a circle round the bowl.

3

The distance between the circle of clay and the bowl determines how thick the sides of the mould will be.

4
Brush oil over all the surfaces where the plaster is to be poured. Check that the clay is firmly pressed down on the glass.

5
Prepare a fairly large quantity of plaster.

6
Sprinkle the plaster onto the water. The mixture should not go lumpy.

7
Cover the bowl with plaster as well as the glass between the bowl and the circle of clay.

8
As the plaster sets, add a little more plaster until it is the required shape and size. Then finish off the surface of the mould.

9
Use a scraper to smooth the entire surface.

10
The clay circle is no longer needed and can be removed.

11
The bottom edge can also be smoothed.

12

Continue tidying up the surface to make the mould the required shape.

13

Use a knife to tidy up the edge. This will prevent the mould from breaking easily, as well as getting rid of irregularities in the surface.

14

The basic model can easily be removed from the mould.

15

Finally smooth out the top with the scraper.

16

The mould is finished and can be used for countless reproductions.

A mould made in two parts

This chapter describes how to make a mould in two parts and the reason why. We have used an existing vase as a basic model, as this can be found in any home.
This particular vase is easy to reproduce because of its round shape.
The end product which is achieved by following the step-by-step instructions is a professional mould which can be used to make as many vases as you wish in clay or in plaster, depending on the materials and facilities available to you.

For any models which are wider at the bottom or in the middle than at the top, you will have to make a mould consisting of two parts.

These two parts are made with a casing for the mould itself, and clay. This casing can simply be made from tin (0.8 mm) and consists of two halves. Make sure that these two halves always overlap slightly or the plaster will leak out. If necessary, stop up the cracks and seams with a little bit of clay. You could also make the casing from wood.

The basic model we have chosen is an exisiting earthenware vase, but as we mentioned above, any shape and material is suitable, provided that you use a separating agent. You can also buy ready-to-use plaster moulds from shops specialising in articles for ceramics. Addresses of these shops can usually be found in the Yellow Pages.

The principle should soon become clear to you if you follow the photographs. A very important aspect of this type of mould are the so-called 'seals'. These ensure that the two halves of the mould are precisely joined together when you are making the plaster cast. The seals are made, as shown in the photographs, using a special type of modelling tool designed especially for the purpose.

These can also be bought in specialist ceramic shops. You can also use a Stanley knife or another sharp knife to make these seals. There are more seals along the edge. These are cut out of the rather hard clay with a knife.

1
The vase is divided into two by a vertical line.

2
Bury the vase in a flat lump of clay as far as the line. Push a lump of clay in the opening of the vase to prevent the plaster going inside.

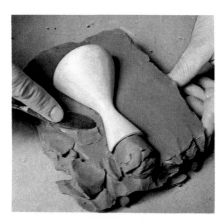

3
Place the tin (0.8 mm) around the lump of clay. The two parts together form a sort of open box.

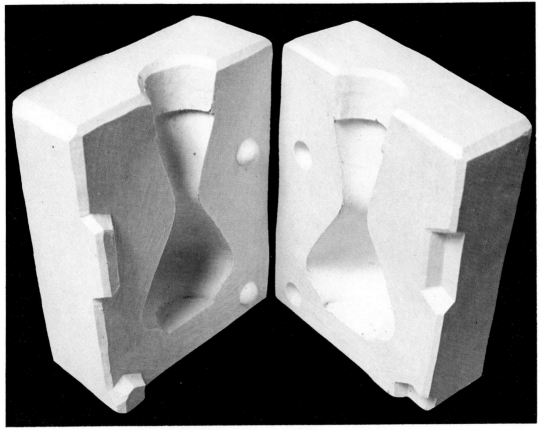

This is a mould in two parts to reproduce a vase. The work itself is attractive, and in addition gives you the possibility of casting as many of these vases as you like.

4

Brush oil over all the surfaces where the plaster is poured.

5

Prepare the plaster and carefully pour in the box (about 5 cm. thick).

6

When the plaster has set, finish off the surface smoothly with a piece of tin or a scraper.

7

When you have finished the surface remove the under layer of clay and the clay stopper for the mouth of the vase.

8

Scrape the entire surface of the plaster with a knife to make it perfectly smooth.

9

Use a sharp modelling tool, hollow pipe or knife and turn in the surface of the plaster to make two hollows or seals.

10

Make two more holes in the edge of the half shape so that the other half of the form will stay in place without any problem.

11

For the second half of the shape, again use the tin casing, brushing oil all over the surfaces which will come into contact with the plaster. Do not forget to close the space resulting from the clay stopper with more clay.

12

Prepare the plaster, pour into the casing and wait for it to set.

13

The second half of the mould is also finished off neatly with the scraper.

14

Two protruding knobs appear in the second half of the mould. These fit exactly over the seals.

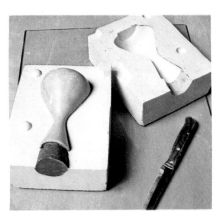

15

Finally clean the inside of the mould thoroughly with soap and water to remove the remaining oil.

A mould in three parts

Now that you know how to make a mould in two parts, you are ready to try a mould in three parts. This type of mould is useful for casting cylindrical models with a hollow base. The third part forms the base of the mould. In this way you can cast a more faithful – as well as a more accurate – copy. The photographs show that two bases are made. One of these serves as a temporary support for the walls of the mould and is destroyed; the other definitive base is the bottom part of the mould. It joins exactly onto the other two parts by means of a seal.

This process incorporates a new technique; that of making a base for the mould. Make a round tin casing that is not very high. Place this cylinder on a base of clay, cover the seams with clay and pour in a sufficient amount of plaster. When the plaster has set slightly, press the basic model firmly into the prepared plaster exactly up to the line drawn earlier. Do not forget to use the separating agent.

When the plaster has set enough for the round mould to remain, the cylinder can be removed. Now the sides are made by making vertical dividing walls. Again work on a glass plate as a base.

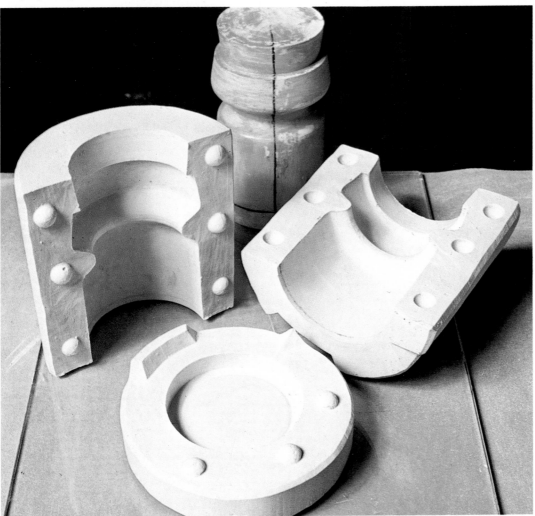

This sort of mould in three parts can be made without any problem if you follow the instructions with the photographs. The resulting mould is particularly suitable for the reproduction of cylindrical models.

1

Draw a vertical line down the model so that it is divided in two, and a horizontal line across, about 2 cm. from the bottom. This provides the thickness of the base.

2

Make a casing from tin and clay and brush oil over all the surfaces which will come into contact with the plaster.

3

Then prepare the plaster and pour it into the small casing.

4

When the plaster has set slightly, press the original model into the plaster as far as the horizontal line, while gently turning it.

5

Leave the plaster to set and remove the model. The surface of the plaster is now smoothed over.

6

Replace the model in the base and brush oil over the parts of the surface which will come into contact with the plaster.

7

Make walls of clay which will serve as a wall to divide the halves when the plaster is poured into the casing.

8

Make a well-sealed, semi-circular casing from tin or another pliable material. Do not forget to seal the bottom thoroughly with clay.

9

Fill the casing until the clay wall is almost entirely covered with plaster. Leave it to set.

10

When the tin is removed, finish off the outside of the mould by smoothing it with a scraper and some sandpaper.

11

Remove the model and make the seals in the same way as described in the previous chapter.

12

Now replace the original in the finished mould with the seals.

13

Brush more oil on the surface where necessary, and again fit on the semi-circular casing. If necessary, secure it with broad elastic bands and seal any gaps and seams with clay.

14

When the plaster has set, remove the tin and the clay and take away the new part (the base) that will no longer be used. Turn over what remains of the mould.

15

Make seals in the two halves of the mould at the bottom. Then make the casing for the base of the mould. Brush oil on the surface where necessary and till the casing with plaster.

16

When the plaster has set remove the casing. There is now a new base with the fittings for the seals. The three parts of the mould are now finished.

Plaster casts consisting of a number of sections

Now that you have made a number of plaster moulds, it is time to practise the actual technique. You can choose between two types of material: plaster itself and the type of clay used for casting. Plaster is suitable for a solid decorative figure which can be worked at a later stage, while clay is suitable for more practical and household articles, but you will need a kiln if you use this material.

Before you make a plaster cast you must take into account some essential factors, but once these have been taken into consideration you cannot really go wrong.

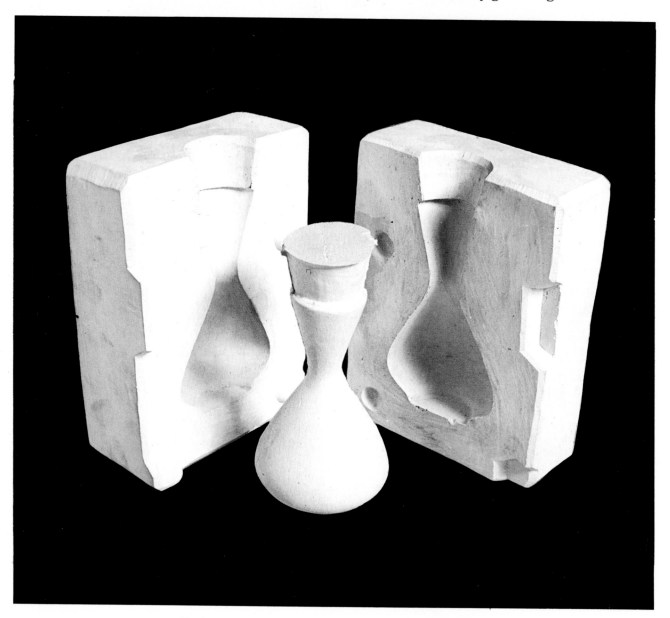

The first plaster cast from the mould described in a previous chapter.

When you are making a plaster cast it is important to prepare the mould properly to ensure that the different parts will not stick together. You now know what separating agents can be used. In this particular case it is necessary to use two agents at a time, i.e., oil and a soap solution. It is also advisable to apply more than just one coat of each.

Nevertheless, despite any preventative measures you take, it sometimes happens that you are unable to separate the plaster parts. Never try to force the plaster out, but carefully tap against the side of the mould with a wooden mallet. This will usually work and the parts will come out. If they do not, pour a little water over the seams. If this does not work

either, try to tap a wooden wedge into a seam with a wooden mallet. Lie the whole mould on a soft surface such as a cushion and try to open the seam very carefully bit by bit. Despite the seals, you will need to hold the plaster parts together with elastic bands. Use wide elastic bands and do not be in a hurry to open the mould.

Curb your impatience to see the results, and wait until the plaster has set quite hard. A sort of stopper appears at the top of the vase where the plaster was poured in. This can be filed off with a hacksaw.

Remember that plaster is a fragile material. Work very carefully, but if pieces break off, they can always be repaired later.

1

Ready to use: the mould described in a previous chapter, liquid soap, oil, a spoon, a bowl of plaster, a paintbrush, a knife, a scraper and a wooden mallet.

2

Brush the two surfaces inside the mould thoroughly with oil.

3

Then apply a coat of soap solution straightaway on the same surface. The soap and oil make it easier for the plaster to come out of the mould later.

4

Close up the mould, and as an extra precaution hold it together with rubber bands.

5

Prepare the plaster and remove the lumps.

6

Check that the mould is properly sealed. Then pour in the plaster.

7

The plaster should be slightly above the top of the mould but it should not run over the side.

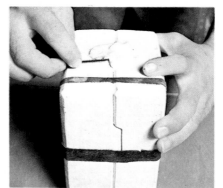

8

When the plaster has almost set, remove the excess with a knife.

9

Wait until the plaster has set hard and then use the scraper until the top of the plaster is just as high as the top edge of the mould.

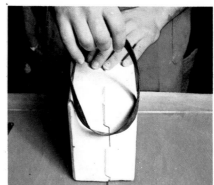

10

When the plaster has set thoroughly, remove the elastic.

A cup made of casting slip

As plaster moulds are primarily meant for the ceramic industry, we include an example of work made with casting slip. The products which are made in this way have to be fired and glazed before they can be used. Not everyone has a kiln, but if you want to have your work fired you can sometimes ask for this to be done in a local school or an arts and crafts centre. However, you have to start by casting the work and this can be fun in itself.

You will discover how much moisture plaster is capable of absorbing.

11
Softly tap the seam of the mould to open it.

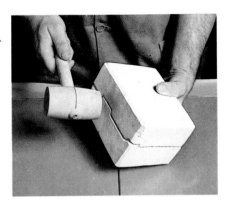

12
This photograph shows the replica inside the open mould.

13
Very carefully remove the replica from the mould. Lift each end at the same time without exerting too much pressure.

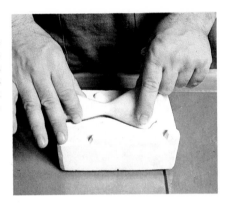

Ready-to-use casting slip
Casting slip can be bought ready to use from shops specialising in pottery articles. This slip can be used as it comes. Simply fill up the mould with it up to the top. You will soon notice the level dropping as a result of the absorbent effect of the plaster. Fill up to the top again. After about ten minutes – depending on how thick the sides of the cup are to be – the liquid slip can be poured out of the mould. Do this with a turning movement so that the inside is as smooth as possible. Leave the mould to drain for a few minutes, if necessary placing it on two sticks over a bucket. Then the cup can be turned right side up. During this process the clay shrinks and the cup can be taken out of the mould. It is important not to be too impatient and it is better to wait a little longer than to take it out too soon. If you wish to fire the cup, cut away the edges with a knife and finish off the whole thing with a wet sponge. The cup should then be left to dry gradually, and little can go wrong with the firing.

1

Requirements: a mould in three parts, a piece of wide elastic to keep the pieces together, and a jug of casting slip.

2

Seal the mould thoroughly with an elastic band around it. Then pour in the liquid slip.

3

Plaster absorbs water. This causes the level of the slip to fall. Fill up with slip up to the top.

4

Pour the slip out of the mould. Some of the slip remains behind on the sides. Repeat this process a few times until the sides are 2 - 3 mm. thick.

5

Now hold the mould upside down over the bowl of slip so that the slip which has not remained behind can drain away.

6

Open the mould and take out the cup. The cup can be smoothed with various modelling tools or a knife.

Reproducing a relief

In previous exercises we mentioned 'carving' a relief. It is also possible to make a plaster cast of this so that the relief can in principle be reproduced endlessly.
This sort of plaster cast is very decorative and in fact the mould itself makes an attractive object to hang on a wall.

Making a mould for a relief is more difficult and requires more practice, but practice makes perfect in the end.
In the first place, a relief must be made on a flat surface. In the example we have used another flower motif. To avoid problems, ensure that only three pieces are used for the mould. Once again separating agents are important. Apart from soap and oil it is also possible to use shellac dissolved in methylated spirits. For this process you also use clay separation walls and a glass plate as a base.

The result of a job that will not produce any problems. The mould is ready to use for making a number of reliefs.

1

Materials: plaster, oil, soap, a paintbrush, a knife, a scraper, a stirring tool, coils of clay, shellac dissolved in methylated spiritis, and the relief.

2

When the shellac is dissolved, the relief is completely covered. The surface should be permeated with this everywhere.

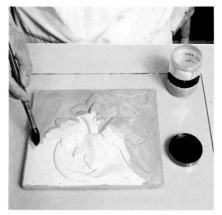

3

When the first coat is dry, apply a second coat. No more of the solution should be able to soak into the surface.

4

Wait for the shellac to dry. Then brush on the soap solution and then the oil on all the parts which come into contact with the plaster.

5

Make clay walls as shown on the photograph and fill the spaces in between with plaster.

6

When the plaster has set, remove the clay. Use a scraper to smooth the surface of the edges in the usual way.

7

Wherever the relief and glass come into contact with the plaster again apply soap and oil (always in that order).

8

Make more clay walls as shown in this photograph and press firmly down on the glass base.

9
Fill the open space between the walls with plaster, making sure that it is the same thickness all the way round.

10
When the plaster has set, remove the clay. Finish off the new surface in the same way as before.

11
Apply a coat of soap and oil to the surface, i.e., the relief, the pieces of plaster now forming a frame and a part of the glass plate.

12
Make a clay wall around the plaster frame. This should be higher than the plaster and be at an equal distance from the border at every point.

13
Now carefully fill this clay frame with plaster to the top. The pieces inside should not slide about.

14
When the plaster has set, remove the clay wall.

15
Use the scraper to finish off the surface. First smooth the edges, then all irregularities in the surface.

Plaster casts consisting of a number of parts

In previous chapters some simple moulds were described.
The more complicated the basic model, the more parts you will need for the mould. This chapter contains a description of how to make a mould consisting of a number of parts, for a classical female head. This can be used to make any number of replicas.

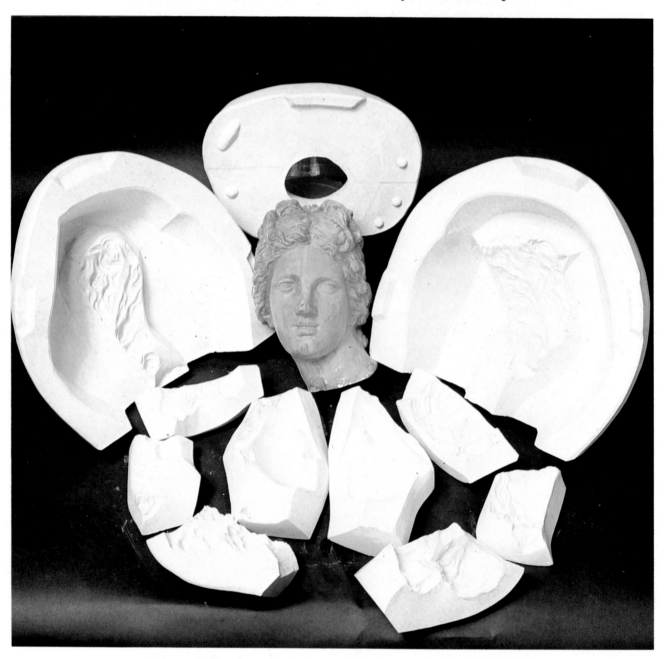

Making a mould for this sort of complicated model looks rather like a jigsaw puzzle.
This sort of mould requires some practice, but the results are certainly worth the effort.

Making this sort of mould is a challenge in itself, and practice makes perfect. You must follow the photographs very carefully and precisely. None of the parts should be smaller or larger than is strictly necessary. It is also important that they fit together perfectly so that the basic model is reproduced as accurately as possible.

The model in our example is a woman's head cast in plaster. Obviously you could use a different model or a different material, depending on what is available, but in principle the procedure remains the same.

The preparation of both the basic model and the separate sections of the mould is again extremely important.

The separating agents discussed in earlier chapters – soap,

oil and shellac – are used. As usual, you work on a glass plate and the dividing walls are made of clay. The principle is as follows: a working base made of plaster containing the head is divided into a number of lines.

'Containers' are made of clay on these lines and these are then filled with plaster. The containers should not be adjacent. The 'puzzle' is built up bit by bit. The centre section is done last of all.

It is also important to finish off the sections properly. They should always taper to a point, i.e., the side should slant. In this way the sections fit together well and the replica will be as accurate as possible.

1

Requirements: soap, oil, shellac, a paintbrush, a knife, a stirrer, a pencil, a saw blade, a piece of thick elastic band, the model, plaster and a bowl.

2

Brush shellac dissolved in methylated spirits all over the model so that it is impermeable.

3

Divide the head in two with a pencil line, as shown in the photograph.

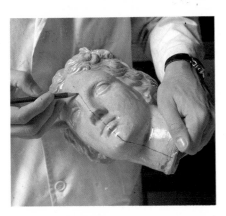

4

Place a clay wall around the model and cut the clay along the pencil line from the top.

5

Make another clay wall, this time at a larger distance from the model. The space created in this way is filled with plaster, and when this has set, it serves as a working basis; it does not in itself form part of the mould that is being made.

6

Continue pouring plaster between the clay walls; the plaster should not be any higher than the edge of the inner clay wall.

7

When the plaster has set, remove the outer clay wall.

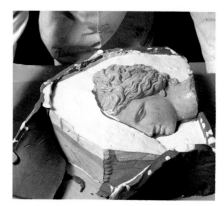

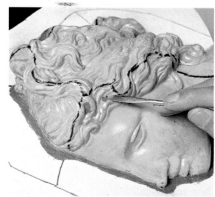

8

Use a saw blade or scraper to smooth the whole surface, removing all the irregular parts.

9

On the plaster indicate how the mould is to be divided into parts. By using a number of parts it is possible to reproduce the model accurately despite the complicated surface.

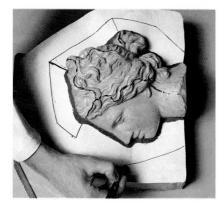

10

Cover the places which might be a problem when the plaster is taken off the model with pieces of clay.

11

Put clay walls around the model, pressing down well, around two non-adjacent areas. The inside of the clay wall should follow the line.

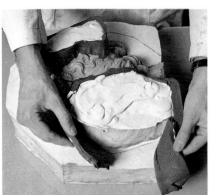

12

Brush soap and oil over the part of the head that comes into contact with the plaster.

13

Carefully pour the plaster into the clay 'container' formed in this way.

14

When the plaster has set, remove the clay walls.

15
Tidy up the pieces with the scraper. Make sure that the walls taper slightly.

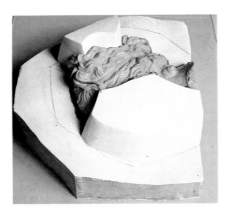

16
The next parts of the mould are also made in this way. Brush oil onto the dividing walls which have already been cast. Keep the central part open for the time being.

17
When you have tidied up the new pieces, make a clay wall around the whole thing and brush soap and oil over the whole model.

18
Pour plaster into the container formed in this way up to the top.

19
Now turn over the mould and remove the working base of plaster.

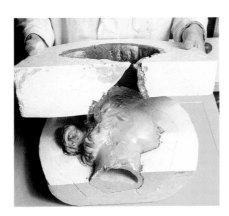

20
Indicate with lines where the parts of the different mould come on the other half of the original.

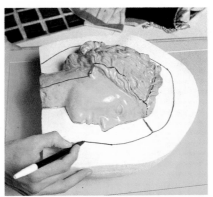

21
Make two more clay containers which are not adjacent and pour liquid plaster in these containers. Do not forget to brush soap and oil on all the parts where plaster is poured.

22
The first two parts have been tidied up and separated from the bottom half. Now do the next two.

23

Tidy up the parts so that the sides taper slightly. This means that they will come free more easily when the plaster has been cast.

24

Indicate where the seals will come on the matrix made earlier (the outside of the half of the mould that is now on the bottom).

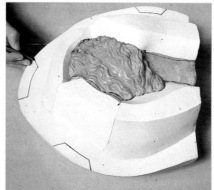

25

Cut out the seals with the knife.

26

Make a clay wall for the other half and pour plaster in this.

27

The two halves of the mould are put together, with the model, bottom up, between them. (See photograph.) The two halves are held together with an elastic band. Now draw the seals for the final piece that is made last.

28

Make the seals with a knife or modelling tool.

29

The whole opening at the bottom of the neck of the model is filled with a lump of clay. This later becomes the channel to pour through.

30

Make another clay wall; the surfaces of the plaster are brushed with soap and oil and the plaster is poured into this container.

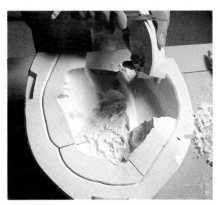

31
The seams between the outer wall of the mould and the separate parts of the mould on the inside must be deepened by making a groove.

32
When the plaster is dry, separate the two matrices, making sure that the inner parts of the mould stay in place.

Things to know about plaster moulds.

There are a number of essential points to remember when you are making a plaster mould. They are enumerated below.

1. *The model. The original object of which a mould is first made so that it can then be used to make a plaster cast. There is a wide choice of materials to do this.*
2. *Separating agents. These ensure that the various parts do not stick together and the model can always be removed.*
3. *Casings. These are used to cast the moulds for the models which are to be reproduced. A number of different materials can be used; metal (e.g., tin, 0.8 mm.), wood, synthetic materials (e.g., linoleum), always with the smooth side turned in.*
4. *Seals. These ensure that the various parts of the mould join together well. They should be rounded off as smoothly as possible or they will soon break off.*
5. *Modelling plaster or casting plaster. This is the best quality plaster to use for making moulds. It's cheaper if you buy it in bulk.*

Modelling with plaster

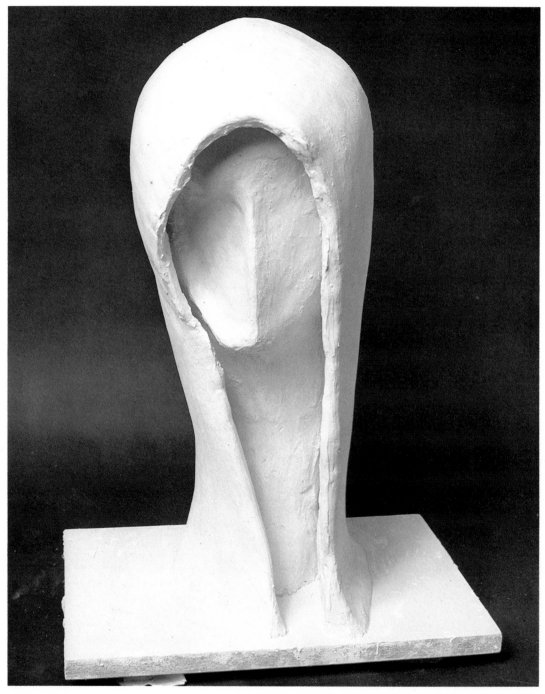

Plaster can be combined with jute to make a medium which can be used to create beautiful sculptures.

Working with plaster and jute is not only fun, but it is actually not as difficult to do as it appears. When the two materials are combined, the result is a medium which can be used to give free rein to your imagination. The great advantage is that the material can be formed into any shape you wish. It is just as easy to remove a little bit as to add a bit, provided that the material is still soft. Another advantage is that you can stick new pieces onto plaster which has already set quite hard. If you do this, you must make sure that the surface is thoroughly wet. Whatever subject you choose, whether it is a bust or a figure of a person or an animal, you must always do the modelling onto a basic structure. This usually consists of wire of different thicknesses. Often welding rods are used to make the inside of this basic structure.

These are attached to a wooden base plate and then thin wire is used to create the required volume or skeleton. It is also possible to use wire mesh for this.

1
Requirements: jute, string, welding rods, wire, scissors, nails and a wooden board.

2
Nail the welding rod to the board with a few nails.

3
Twist the thin wire round the welding rod in a spiral from the top downwards to create the required figure.

4
The frame for this figure is ready and the plaster can be prepared.

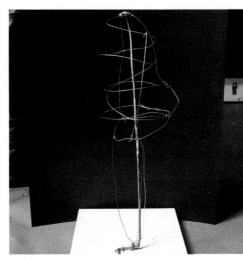

With regard to the jute there is a choice between various different sorts. For smaller projects it is best to use a fairly fine type of jute. Jute can be bought in different coarsenesses from shops selling artists' materials or specialising in window-dressing. Do not buy an expensive quality. In this case it is best to use the cheaper plasterer's plaster. The thickness is about the same as that used for plaster casts, i.e., roughly the same consistency as yoghurt.

Few or no special tools
Apart from the most important tools, your own hands, you will only need a few modelling tools, which can be bought in shops which sell artists' materials. These are used to create the desired shape. Finally the figure has to be given a smoothsurface. This is done with sandpaper, and for finishing off the coarse details it is best to use a file.

It is only possible to finish off smoothing the surface with a file or sandpaper when the figure has set properly.
You should take some safety precautions as sanding off plaster is an extremely dusty business. If possible, it is best to work outside, or on a balcony or in a garage.
Also make sure that you brush your feet thoroughly before you go inside or the house will be covered in plaster dust before you know where you are.

5
Now cut the jute into strips to cover the wire frame.

6
The strips of jute are dipped into the prepared plaster.

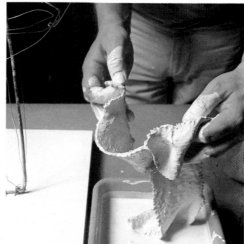

7
When the jute has been soaked in plaster, cover the wire frame with it.

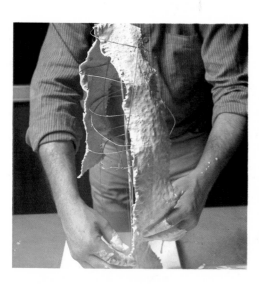

8
When you have added a few more strips of plaster, leave them to set for a while.

9 An extra layer of jute is wrapped around the base as this has to support the entire weight of the figure.

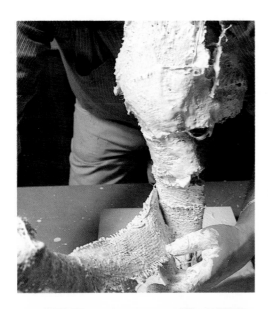

10 When the plaster and jute mixture has set, it is possible to add more plaster without jute with your hands. The surface is now quite hard.

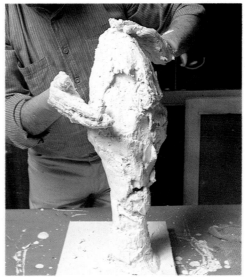

11 Where necessary, apply some more jute soaked in plaster.

12 The features are now formed with the hand.

13 The final shape is now emerging and it is time to take a really critical look at the figure.

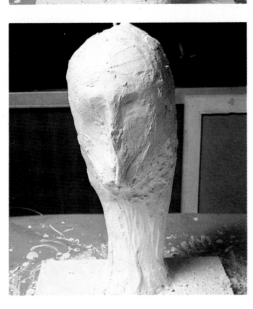

14 Using a modelling tool, sculpt the features more clearly while the plaster is still fairly soft.

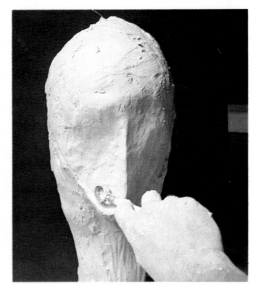

15

Now the head scarf is made. To make this build a frame of wire and rope. The rope is used to suggest natural folds in the cloth.

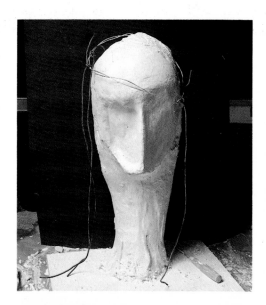

16

Prepare some more plaster and continue in the usual way. The surface of the figure should be wetted first.

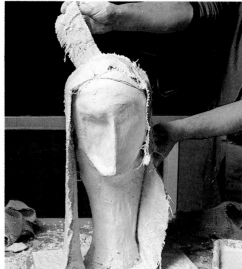

17

Where the headscarf is to be, apply strips of jute soaked in plaster.

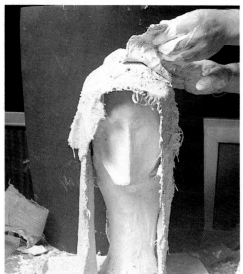

18

Then wait until the plaster has set slightly.

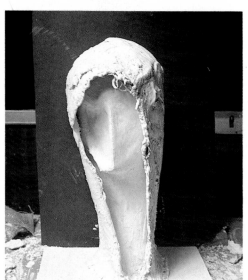

19

Using only plaster and a knife, add the final details and smooth the surface as much as possible.

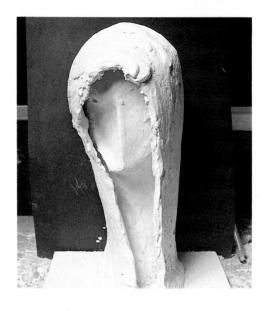

20

When the plaster has set thoroughly, a file and sandpaper are used to produce the final shape required.

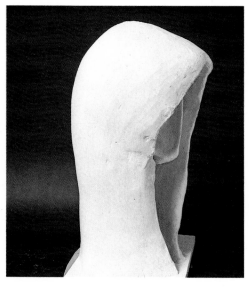

An imitation lead elephant

With the right ingredients you can change a plaster cast into an imitation lead figure. This is fun to do and the results are extremely attractive.

Not only is it fun to decorate your plaster figures, but in this way you can also make some very attractive ornaments.

On the following pages you can find out how to turn a plaster elephant into one that looks as though it is made of lead. The final product is surprisingly realistic.
You probably have some of the ingredients at home, but if not, they are very easy to obtain.

1 Materials: graphite powder, asphalt, lacquer, wax, black vinyl emulsion paint, turpentine based oil, brushes, fine sandpaper, a primus stove, the elephant and a set of tusks made of real or imitation ivory.

2 Start by sanding the whole elephant down.

3 When you have sanded down the entire surface, apply a layer of black silk finish emulsion paint.

4 Check that the elephant is entirely covered in paint and then wait for it to dry.

5 Now pour three parts of turpentine based oil into an empty jar and add the following ingredients.

6 Add one part of wax and stir to make a homogeneous mixture.

7 Stirring constantly with a paintbrush or another utensil, heat the mixture au bain marie.

8 When the mixture is completely liquid and homogeneous, add a little bit of asphalt.

9 Sprinkle some graphite powder on a piece of cloth; approximately the amount shown in the photograph.

10 First dip the paintbrush in the mixture of turpentine oil and wax, and then rub the graphite powder to make a thick paste.

11 The paste should be brushed all over the elephant, leaving no part uncovered.

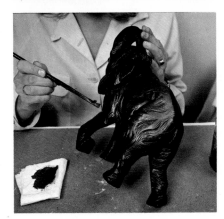

12 When the paste is dry, rub the elephant to a shine with a soft cloth.

13 Finally, stick down the tusks and the elephant is ready.

Colouring the plaster

Aparts from the method described above used to give the plaster an imitation colour, there are a number of other possibilities, some of which are well-known, others of which are not. A few of these methods are described below.

1. *A dry plaster model can be made to look like wood, and is almost indistinguishable from the real thing, simply by varnishing it with wax or wood stain.*
2. *A plaster figure will look quite different when it is painted with gold, silver or bronze paint. These paints can be bought in either liquid or solid form in shops specialising in artists' materials or pottery.*
3. *In a previous chapter there was an explanation of how plaster can also be painted with watercolours. The plaster is then covered with a layer of transparent varnish.*

4. *A less well-known method that is sometimes used is to finish the figure off in a shade of ivory. This is done as follows: heat the plaster figure in the oven. Melt a large quantity of stearic acid in a container and lie the heated figure in this for about five minutes. When it has cooled down, polish it with a soft brush.*

Protecting the plaster
If the plaster is not coloured, it will eventually become very dusty. If you spray the piece once or twice with hair lacquer, this will make it easier to clean as the dust is unable to penetrate the plaster.

A turning box for a vase

The turning box is an old-fashioned device which can be used to make almost any solid plaster cast. The actual shape of the plaster cast can be any shape you wish.
You can demonstrate your artistic talents using this method, as well as your skill in working with plaster. The photographs show the steps in this process.

This solid vase is certainly not difficult to make, provided that you follow the instructions which accompany the photographs.

Sometimes you may wish to design your very own model. This is very easy to do using a potter's wheel. If you don't have a wheel, it's also possible to use a turning box. This is easy to make yourself and the end product is exactly the same. The principle on which it operates is that a rotating axis is covered with liquid plaster to form a central core. This core is then literally shaved into the correct shape using a mould.

The box consists of a rectangular wooden frame with a rotating axis made from a welding rod. This needs to be secured on either side so that it does not move at all while it is turning. Use rubber rings to secure the rod. Slide these around the rod again on both sides of the box.

A plaster core is cast around this axis and this is formed into the correct shape by the mould. The mould should be made of metal, preferably tin (0.8 mm.) or aluminium. Cut the required shape from the sheet of tin with a pair of tin shears. The shape is first drawn to size on a sheet of paper and then transferred onto the metal with carbon paper. Go over the lines with a waterproof felt tip pen to make sure that they are quite clear. This makes it easy to cut out the shape. Now nail the profile onto a wooden stick with a few nails, exactly in between the two short sides of the box which is again nailed down.

The core of rope or jute
To make sure the liquid plaster adheres to the core at the beginning, you need to wind some material around the rod. There are a number of different possiblities.

First, you can wind some jute around the rod, securing it with thin wire. It is also possible to use sisal instead of jute. By passing some pieces of wire or reed through the sisal or jute, you can make a sort of barbed wire core.

Now you are ready to start making your model. Everywhere the plaster should not stick to the core should be covered with liquid soap. As usual you should work on a glass plate. The liquid plaster, not too thin, should be poured around the core as it is turning round. If you need to apply more plaster later on, wet the surface of the core first and score it in various places with a knife. This will make it easier for the next layer to remain stuck down.

Finally, the layer of plaster will become so thick that it touches the profile of the metal mould. This now produces the actual shape of the figure. Continue adding plaster until the figure is the required shape. To obtain a really smooth surface, the last layer of plaster should be fairly thin. When the plaster has set, carefully remove the rod. This technique is a matter of practising as long as it takes to obtain the required results.

1

Make a frame from a few pieces of wood. The rotating axis is fixed onto the frame.

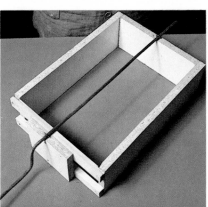

2

The vase is made lengthways in the frame. To do this you must measure the centre point on each of the two short sides. Bore two holes in these two sides.

3

Pass the rod through the two hoops.

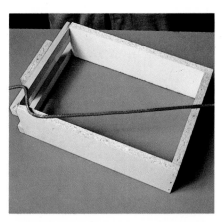

4

Draw the outline of the vase on a sheet of white paper.

5

Transfer this outline onto a metal plate with carbon paper; the metal should preferably be tin or aluminium.

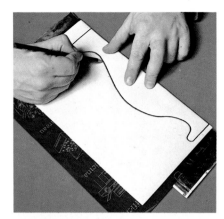

6

Cut out the profile.

7

Nail the 'negative' profile onto a piece of wood with a few small nails.

8

The piece of wood is now secured onto the frame with a few nails in such a way that the ends of the metal are flush with the rod.

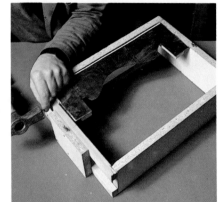

9

Now wrap a piece of coarse jute, sisal or another material around the end of the rod and rotate the rod to wind it all the way round.

10

Secure the whole thing with a piece of wire, rotating the rod all the time.

11

The rod is clamped down with two rubber rings in such a way that it cannot move.

12

Now brush oil over the part of the rod that is not covered with material to prevent the plaster from sticking to it.

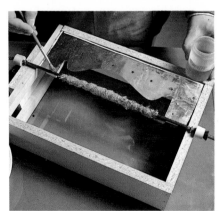

13

Place the frame on a glass plate and gradually apply the plaster to the material.

14

Rotate the rod slowly, all the while continuing to add plaster.

15

Every time new plaster has to be added, make a few grooves in the first layer and wet it so that the second layer adheres more effectively.

16

Continue adding plaster with a spoon. The figure gradually becomes thicker.

17

The rotating plaster eventually reaches the metal profile and starts to assume this shape.

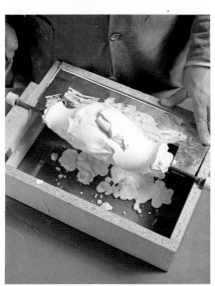

18

Constantly check the figure and add plaster whenever this is needed.

19
If you rotate the figure, you can see where more plaster is needed.

20
The narrowest parts of the vase are the most difficult to shape.

21
Perfect the shape of the vase, constantly rotating it.

22
Continue adding plaster whenever necessary.

23
Do not stop rotating; the shape will continue to improve.

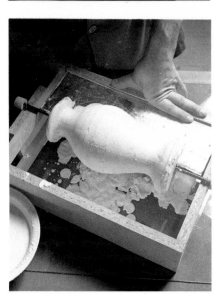

24
When the vase is almost finished, the plaster should be thin enough to cover all the remaining flaws.

25

Continue rotating until the surface cannot become any smoother.

26

Lastly, finish off the ends. They should be perfectly flat and smooth.

27

The vase is now finished.

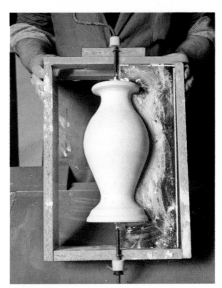

28

Bend the hoops with a pair of pliers and remove the vase from the frame on its rod.

29

Place the vase on a piece of material or on a towel and tap against the end of the rod with a hammer to loosen it.

30

Finally remove the rod without damaging the vase.

Making a relief on the vase

The previous chapter described how to make a smooth vase using a rotating frame. We have also described how to make a relief pattern on a smooth plate. As you will see, this technique is also very suitable for use on a round figure. It is also possible to decorate the vase by adding decorative patterns to the surface, rather than by cutting them out. The result is the same – an attractively decorated solid vase which can serve as a decoration, or otherwise as a mould for another plaster case.

The vase made using a rotating frame has been decorated with an interesting original relief pattern. If necessary, it can be used to cast a mould.

1 Requirements: the vase, chisels and gouges, a pencil, drawing paper and a pair of compasses.

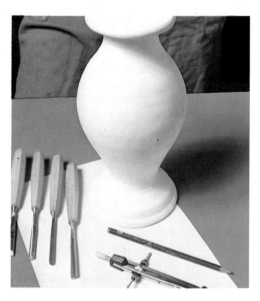

2 For the design of the motif draw half of the vase onto a sheet of paper.

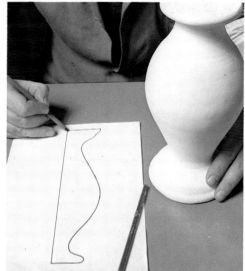

3 Using a piece of string, measure the circumference of the part of the vase to be decorated. In this way you can work out what size the motif should be and how far apart the circles should be from each other.

4 When you have worked out the size and spacing of the motifs and drawn them on the profile, measure the radius with a pair of compasses.

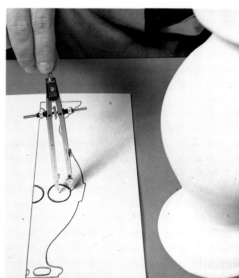

5 Transfer this size onto the vase with the compasses and draw the outer ring.

6 Draw a smaller concentric circle inside this ring.

7
The motif on the lip of the vase is made using the same method.

8
This is followed by motifs for the foot.

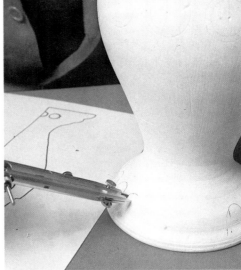

9
Cut out the parts of the lip indicated in this way using a flat chisel.

10
Then cut away the plaster around the motifs in the middle. These seem to lie on the surface of the vase.

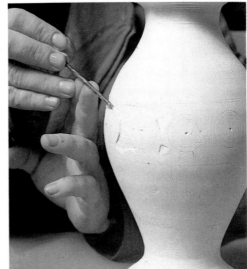

11
Turn the vase upside down so that it is easier to get to the bottom of the motifs.

12
Do the motifs on the foot of the vase in the same way.

13 Again use a small flat chisel for these motifs.

14 The motifs stand out very clearly on the surface of the plaster. This is followed by the details of the work; use a gouge to do these.

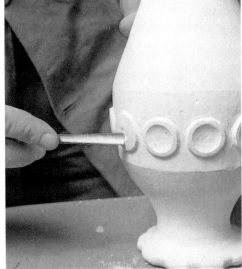

15 The motifs around the foot of the vase should be rounded off as much as possible with a chisel or gouge.

16 Make all the details smooth with sandpaper.

17 The motifs on the foot are treated in the same way.

18 The rounded sides are also smoothly sanded down.

19
Finally, the rim is sanded and all the sides and corners are made quite smooth.

Tips for working with plaster

1. *Gluing back broken pieces.*
   Plaster is a fragile material and bits can easily break off a work. These cannot really be glued back because of the structure of the plaster.
   It is only really possible to stick pieces of plaster back by using plaster, viz., by making the surfaces wet and applying a layer of liquid plaster. The surfaces should then be pressed together and the remaining liquid plaster should be spread over the cracks. Then remove excess plaster with a wet sponge. When the plaster has set, sand down with sandpaper.

2. *Plaster casts can be made in virtually any material. If you look around you can find dozens of objects in your home which could serve as a model for the plaster cast.*
   For example, cake tins with a detachable base are very suitable for casting a circular base, and these in turn are very useful for turning.
   In addition, there are plastic bowls and beakers, cardboard cylinders, earthenware pots, sand and jelly moulds. Through experimenting you will discover that the possiblities are virtually limitless.

3. *Plaster is extremely absorbent and a model or mould can only be used between four and six times. After this it has to dry out in a warm place for a few days.*

4. *Plaster should not be lumpy or there will be air bubbles and these cause holes to appear in the finished product. However, it is possible for air bubbles to form in a plaster cast even if you have taken all the necessary precautions and the surface, which should have been perfectly smooth, still has holes in it. These can be removed as follows. First they should be slightly enlarged with a small gouge so that they can be easily filled in.*
   Then make the surrounding area quite wet and fill the holes in which the plaster has already started to set. Finally sand down the whole area.

5. *In an earlier chapter it was suggested that plaster is very suitable as a material for modelling.*
   For this it is used in combination with jute. An excellent alternative is the ready-to-use plaster on gauze. The gauze is actually filled with plaster. When it is wet, it more or less assumes the shape of the object to which it is applied. Jute soaked in plaster has the same properties as plaster gauze, but plaster gauze has a number of advantages. It is much quicker and cleaner to use. In fact you might almost be able to work with it at the living room table. You can buy plaster gauze in well-stocked shops selling artists' materials, and sometimes it is available at chemists'.

6. *An ornament looks best if it is finished off as smoothly as possible. For this you can use sandpaper or wire wool.*

7. *If you intend to make a number of plaster casts, you will find that it is cheaper to buy 50 kilos at a time from a specialist ceramic shop.*

8. *It is very useful to have an adjustable wooden frame when you are making plaster casts. It is easy to make this yourself. The illustrations below show a number of possible alternatives.*

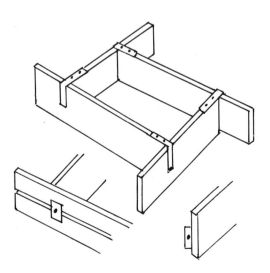

Special tools and an adapted turntable

The preceding chapters have described a number of moulds. By now you should be fairly skilful in working with plaster and have a basic knowledge of the processes involved. The following pages show you how to familiarise yourself with a new and more professional technique, viz., modelling on a turntable. To do this you will need an electric potter's wheel. Below there is a description of how to adapt this for plaster turning with a few simple adjustments and what special tools you will need for this.

In the first place you will need an electric wheel and the best thing to use is an electric potter's wheel.

A few simple adjustments and it is quite suitable for using with plaster, while you can also continue to use it to do pottery.

There is a wide variety of electric potters' wheels on the market.

The type used in our example is a fairly common type.

You will have to alter the metal turntable. Drill about four holes into the disc and then screw nuts and bolts through these holes. The plaster base which serves as a basis for all the other works you turn is cast on this. This plaster base is made using a metal casing and is cast directly onto the disc. A number of grooves are turned into this to ensure that the works you turn remain firmly in place. The nucleus of the model you turn is always cast onto the plaster disc, and when you have finished the model it is cut off.

The plaster disc should then be smoothed off so that it can be used for another work. As you remove a little bit of the disc each time it is used, it may sometimes be necessary to replace it. This should not really present any problems. The simple diagram on p. 67 shows a cross section of a disc with a plaster base. The drawn model does not refer to an electric wheel but merely serves to explain the principle. The photographs also help to explain how it works.

1 Remove the turntable from a normal electric potter's wheel so that it can be adapted for working with plaster.

2 Drill a few holes – three or four – in the turntable in a symmetrical pattern.

3 Pass the bolts through these holes and secure with nuts on either side. This helps to keep the plaster in place.

Special turning tools
In addition to the adapted turntable, you will also need some special turning tools. These include cutting tools with different shaped ends such as a rectangular end, a half moon, a pointed or triangular end. You can use these to make any shape you wish. The tool you use depends on the shape of the object you are making, and it is often a matter of trial and error. In addition to the turning tools, you will also need a hardwood pair of compasses and a few modelling tools. It is best to use tools made of stainless steel.

4

The turntable is put back into place.

5

Place a piece of tin around the turntable and tie a piece of string or an elastic band around it. Then fill the container formed in this way with plaster.

6

When the surface of the plaster has set, sand it and make some grooves in it; these help to keep the work securely positioned on the base.

7

The tools needed for turning have been mentioned a number of times. This is a range of some of the tools used, consisting almost exclusively of cutting tools, each of which has a different shape and is suitable for a specific purpose. There is also a pair of compasses and a modelling tool. You do not need any other instruments for turning plaster models.

Geometric figures on a wheel

When you have adapted the wheel, you can start on some easy turning exercises. As the wheel can only be used to make geometric shapes, this chapter describes how to turn the three most important of these in plaster: a sphere, a cone and a cylinder. The following chapters deal with increasingly complicated shapes based on these figures.

Turning plaster is not only a time-consuming and exacting task, but also requires some skill and experience. Thus you should not imagine that your first attempts will be an immediate success. Anyone who has some experience in turning wood or clay will get the hang of it sooner than someone who is using a wheel for the first time.

It takes a while to learn to use an electric wheel, but practice makes perfect.

Special tools
Using this method of making models is quite similar to the industrial production line process. You start by making a mould of the model so that it is possible to make reproductions quickly and in large numbers.

In addition to the adapted wheel, you will also need some special turning tools. These are described on p. 65 and p. 66.

Learning how to use these is a matter of experience. You will need a rounded rod as a guide in order to use the turning tools properly. This rod is placed against a fixed point at one end. This may be a piece of softboard or a piece of wood. The photographs clearly show how it is used.

The principle can be briefly summarised as follows: the core, which is always a cylinder for the shape to be turned, is cast directly onto the plaster base, and when the plaster has set, it is turned in the desired shape. The following tools are essential: turning tools, a pair of compasses, a paper mould and wet and dry sandpaper.

It is best for the object to be removed from the mould when the plaster is still warm, i.e., after about 1 1/2 to 2 hours. If the figure is the desired shape, it can be sawn off the next piece of work when it has been smoothed off.

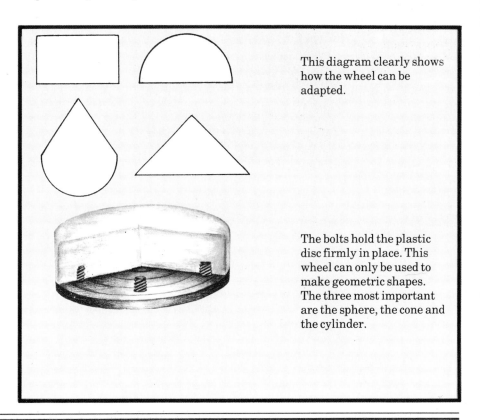

This diagram clearly shows how the wheel can be adapted.

This shows the three geometric figures shown in this exercise: the sphere, the cone and the cylinder.

The bolts hold the plastic disc firmly in place. This wheel can only be used to make geometric shapes. The three most important are the sphere, the cone and the cylinder.

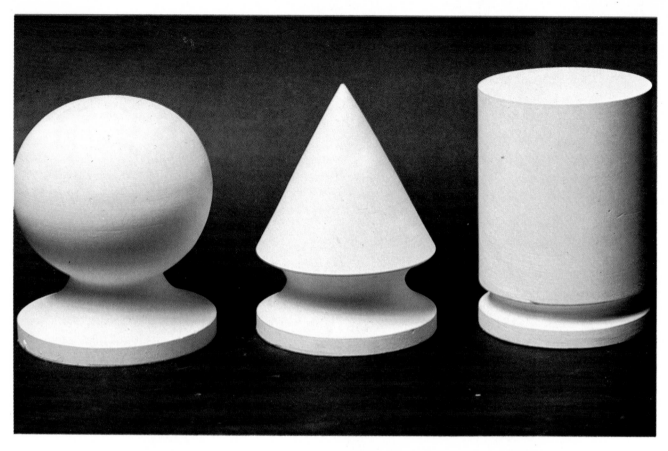

The cylinder

1

Requirements: tin, elastic, potter's plaster, tools, a pencil, a pair of compasses, sandpaper, a rod with a nail at one end.

2

As the wheel is turning, draw a circle on the plaster base.

3

Make a tin casing. Put an elastic band around it and place it on the plaster base, securing it with a coil of clay.

4

Pour plaster into the casing. When it has set, undo the elastic and remove the tin.

5

Press the end of the rod with the nail into the softboard. Hold the cutting tool with the half-moon shaped end against the rod and start removing plaster as the wheel is turning.

6

Continue removing plaster, pressing down evenly until the cylinder has the diameter required.

7

Support the pencil with the rod. Hold the pencil against the cylinder and indicate where the base will be and where the cylinder itself ends.

8

Remove the plaster between the cylinder itself and the base or bottom part.

9

Pressing the blade of the saw into the bottom line, cut through the plaster.

10

It is not necessary to cut the piece entirely free. When the cut is deep enough, a few gentle taps will remove the cylinder from the base.

The cone

1
Again place a piece of tin on the plaster base. Secure with clay and fill up with plaster.

2
Remove the tin. Hold the cutting tool alongside the rod and turn the wheel to remove the excess plaster.

3
Indicate the part of the cylinder that needs to be removed. Use a pencil supported by the rod.

4
Now remove the plaster, starting from the top of the cylinder, until it turns into a cone.

5
Keep the rod in position to form the pointed shape of the cone.

6
Now use the cutting tool with the half-moon blade to remove plaster above the base.

7
Keep turning the wheel until you have the exact shape you require.

8
Carefully sand the whole surface.

9

The cone is ready and can be cut away from the base with a saw.

1

Make a casing, fill it with plaster and wait until it has set.

De sphere

2

Use the pair of compasses to measure the sphere on the side of the cylinder.

3

Indicate the size with a pencil on the cylinder and draw another line to show where the base is.

4

Hold the cutting tool against the rod with your hand and start removing plaster from the top of the cylinder.

5
Remove plaster alternately from the top and the bottom, working towards the centre.

6
Use the most suitable cutting tool for removing the plaster at each particular stage.

7
To get a really rounded shape, press the cutting tool very lightly against the plaster.

8
Carefully sand the entire surface of the sphere, as well as the base, with sandpaper.

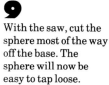

9
With the saw, cut the sphere most of the way off the base. The sphere will now be easy to tap loose.

The first projects on the wheel

The preceding exercises were concerned with making geometric shapes. The practical experience you have gained in doing these will stand you in good stead in the following projects: two figures which are made using a cardboard profile. The core of plaster is turned to the desired shape by this method.

This shows two vases based on an original design, made with the traditional turning tools.

Starting with the same adapted turntable you again use the same tools, as well as the guiding rod. The models are made using a profile. This is first drawn to size, transferred onto thin card, and then cut out. It is used to constantly check the shape until you have achieved the desired result. It takes quite a lot of practice and a steady hand to capture the

drawn model in plaster. The lines of the plaster should be kept as fluid as possible. Again the core is cast on the plaster base.

1
Draw the vase you wish to reproduce on paper. You will need the wheel and the same tools as before.

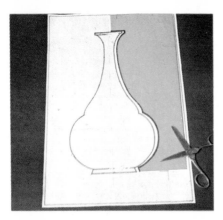

2
On a piece of thin card draw one half of the (symmetrical) vase, and cut it out.

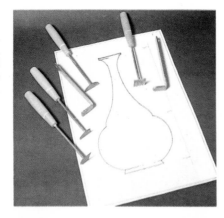

3
Check that the cardboard profile fits properly.

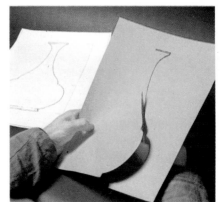

4
Make a tin casing on a plaster base.

5
The casing is secured with string and a coil of clay so that it cannot move. Pour the plaster into the casing.

6
When the plaster has dried, remove the clay and the tin casing.

7

The cylinder of plaster is now ready. Hang the drawing of the vase on the wall behind it.

8

Remove plaster with a suitable cutting tool held against the rod.

9

The neck of the vase is made by tapering the top.

10

Use a different cutting tool for each part of the profile and hold firmly against the rod.

11

Gradually make the definitive shape of the neck, using the drawing as a guide.

12

Use the cardboard profile whenever necessary to check how much the shape is deviating from the design.

13

To produce the correct rounded shape for the vase, remove the plaster from the middle and bottom alternately.

14

Holding the rod firmly, turn the foot of the vase until it is exactly like the design.

15
Finally use sandpaper to sand the entire vase.

16
Check the shape of the vase against the profile for the last time.

17
Now cut the plaster a little bit below the rounded part of the vase to make a foot.

18
Carefully remove the vase from the plaster base and if necessary, sand the foot smooth.

1

Draw the profile of the vase and make the plaster cylinder in the usual way.

2

When the plaster has set, remove the tin casing and the coil of clay.

3

The rod should not be allowed to move. For this reason it is a good idea to bang a nail into the end resting against the wall.

4

Keeping a careful eye on the pattern hanging up behind the wheel and with a firm grip on the rod, start removing the plaster, using the right cutting tool.

5

Form the neck and give it a clear edge.

6

Work down with the cutting tool to give the vase its rounded shape.

7

Remove the excess plaster from the edge with the saw and tidy up the profile.

8

When the vase is ready, sand it smooth.

9 Make a deep cut in the foot of the vase with the blade of a saw.

10 Carefully tap against the vase with your fist so that the vase can be removed from the base.

A turned jug

This chapter not only deals with a new design, but also describes a special technique for making the handle and spout. The photographs clearly show how this is done.

This photograph shows a jug made using a wheel. The main part, handle and spout are all made individually and then joined together. It is possible to use this as a model for a mould.

Some plaster enthusiasts may have felt rather dubious about starting on this series of exercises with the wheel. In the first place, they may have wondered how to obtain the special wheel for turning the plaster, and in the second place, they may have had doubts about the practical use of the objects shown here. With regard to the first point, there certainly are special plaster wheels, but an amateur can easily make do with the traditional potter's wheel with a few adaptations. With regard to the second point, it is not possible to regard working with plaster separately from the intention, i.e., to make reproductions. It is true that on a wheel it is only possible to make solid objects, but it is possible to make moulds from these models using plaster, and these can then be used to make plaster casts of your own designs, and these can be hollow.

The handle and the spout are made separately
The preparations for this jug are the same as those used before, as are the tools required. Because you can make only geometric shapes on the wheel, you must make additions such as handles and the spout separately, and then attach them to the model which has already been completed. By casting the plaster for these separate atachments around a piece of twisted wire, you can make them stronger.

Obviously you will have to use clay when you are casting the separate attachments, as shown in earlier chapters.

1 Place a piece of tin on the plaster base and secure with a coil of clay. Then pour plaster into the casing.

2 When the plaster has set, remove the tin casing. You are now ready to start on the project.

3 The rod is held against the wall at the back. Start removing the plaster with a cutting tool.

4 The jug is taking shape. Use a square ended cutting tool to hollow out the inner part of the top section.

5 Now use sandpaper to make the jug quite smooth. This completes the first stage of the project.

6 Make the lid of the jug from a new plaster cylinder.

7
Use the most suitable cutting tool for every separate part of the project.

8
When the lid is almost finished, carefully measure the diameter of the 'opening' where it has to fit.

9
Continue removing plaster until the lid fits exactly in the opening.

10
Use one of the cutting tools to indicate where the lid has to be cut off.

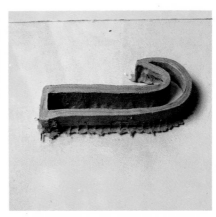

11
Use a piece of wire to cut off the lid along the line that has been drawn.

12
Make a clay wall in the shape of the handle and press down firmly.

13
Twist together two pieces of wire and bend the thick twisted wire in such a way that it fits inside the handle shape.

14
Press the ends of the wire through the clay wall. Lie the wire itself inside the shape.

15
Fill the form with liquid plaster to the top. The wire should be completely covered.

16
Make another clay wall and bend in the shape of a spout. Pass a twisted piece of wire through the middle of the straight piece.

17
Fill the clay container with plaster and wait for both parts – the handle and spout – to set.

18
Use a knife to make the handle the required thickness.

19
Do the same for the spout. Remove excess plaster so that the end tapers to a point.

20
Hold the handle against the jug and show exactly where the holes have to be drilled.

21
Make the holes in these places with an awl.

22
Put some plaster in the holes, pass the ends of the wire there and finish off the whole thing smoothly. Do the same for the spout. Then sand the places where you have put on the handle and the spout.

Making a soup tureen

By now you should have experimented with various exercises, turning the plaster models. Now it's time to try a more complicated project, such as this soup tureen with a lid.
The two parts are made separately, though you must never forget that they make a whole when you have finished.

A soup tureen with a lid that fits, made on the wheel in two stages. The mould is made from this model at a later stage, but this is not described in this chapter.

It takes quite a lot of patience and precision to create a fine classical shape for the tureen. The main thing is to get a smooth surface and to ensure that the two parts are rounded in a complementary fashion. Always use the correct cutting tool and remove the plaster very carefully. It is possible to correct an error by removing a little more plaster, but it is not possible to erase a very deep groove. The tureen and the lid are turned from two separate cylinders. It is very important that the two parts fit exactly. This requires precision work and constant checking.

1
Make a plaster base on the turntable and carve circles in the surface so that the tureen is securely placed on the base.

2
Put a piece of tin around the plaster base and pour plaster in.

3
When the plaster has set, remove the tin. The plaster cylinder made in this way is now worked.

4
Hold the cutting tool against the rod and press firmly against the supporting wall. Now start removing the plaster.

5
Continue removing plaster from the top of the cylinder until the required shape is achieved.

6
Use a suitable cutting tool to make the rounded shape of the knob of the lid.

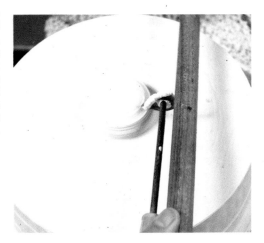

7
Continue turning the plaster until the final shape of the lid is achieved.

8
Now tidy up the edge and go over the entire surface of the lid lightly and carefully.

9
Make the bottom part of the lid (which fits inside the tureen) so that it goes in. This is where the lid is cut off from the base with a nylon wire.

10
The lid is finished. If necessary, sand smooth.

11
Cut off the lid at the indicated place with a nylon wire or the blade of a saw.

12

Place the tin back on the base and tie a piece of string around it. Fill the casing with plaster.

13

When the plaster has set, start turning.

14

Make a profile of the top of the tureen and remove plaster to make the edge.

15

Make the rounded shape of the tureen.

16

Use a knife to indicate where to make the foot of the tureen. Start on this shape.

17

Remove plaster from the opening in the top of the tureen with the most suitable cutting tool, until it is deep enough.

18 Make the indentation above the foot so that the foot is pronounced.

19 To obtain a perfectly smooth and shiny surface, go over the entire tureen, including the foot.

20 The last step should be done extremely carefully to avoid any damage to the surface.

21 If the rim around the top is still too thick, take away as much as is necessary.

22 Measure the diameter of the bottom part of the lid with a pair of compasses to find out whether it fits the inside of the opening of the tureen.

23 When the opening of the tureen is the same diameter as the bottom of the lid, stop removing plaster.

24
Check that the two parts fit perfectly. The lid should fit exactly in the tureen.

25
Now indicate where the tureen should be cut off the base.

26
Cut the tureen off the base with the nylon wire.

A vase consisting of three parts

A vase with a foot and a lid. The three parts, made individually on the wheel, form a harmonious ensemble.

Plaster is easy to turn on a wheel to make a virtually infinite range of geometric shapes.
The elegant vase shown on these pages is a good example.

Within the geometric limitations, there are two possiblities: the first is to turn a shape from one core piece, the plaster cylinder, which is cut off from the base in one piece.
For the second possibility the various parts should be made separately and then joined together to make a whole.
For the vase in three parts shown here consisting of a lid, vase and a foot, you constantly have to use a pair of compasses as well as the diagram of your design with the correct sizes. In this way each part is made exactly to size and the three separate parts will fit together perfectly. The parts are joined together with a thin plaster mixture after making the surfaces very wet.
Make sure that as little plaster as possible is left on the outside. If this does happen, clean with a wet sponge.
The result will be a beautifully made vase which can be decorated with a relief pattern if desired, and can then be made into a mould also consisting of a number of parts.

1
Draw the design for the vase on a sheet of paper. The three parts should be clearly shown with the sizes.

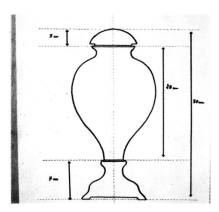

2
Make the plaster base and put on the rings in the usual way.

3
Make a cylindrical casing from a sheet of tin. Place on the plaster base and fill with plaster.

4
When the plaster has set remove the casing. Now measure the greatest width of the vase.

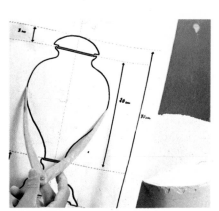

5

Use the compasses to indicate this width on the top of the cylinder. Use a pencil to draw the circle of the same size.

6

Remove the excess plaster until the cylinder has the required diameter.

7

Now measure the outer diameter of the top lip on the diagram with the compasses.

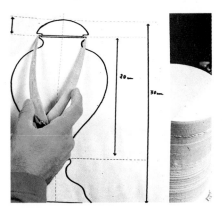

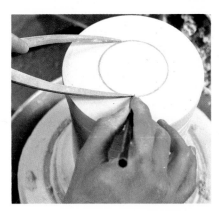

8

Again show this size on the cylinder and draw the circle with a pencil.

9

Press the cutting tool firmly against the rod and then hold it steadily against the wall. Now start to draw the shape of the piece.

10

If necessary, the vase can be decorated with a relief pattern at a later stage. This will be easier if, at this stage, a ridge is made at a suitable height.

11

Continue giving the piece the required shape, going onto the bottom half.

12

Then finish off the top. The lid will have to fit perfectly.

13
If necessary, finish off the main part of the vase and cut off the base.

14
Make a new plaster cylinder. Measure the widest part of the foot of the vase with the compasses.

15
Show this size on top of the plaster cylinder with the compasses and a pencil.

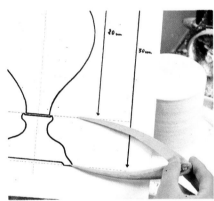

16
Remove plaster until the cylinder has the required diameter.

17
Use the compasses to check that the diameter is the same as that on the diagram.

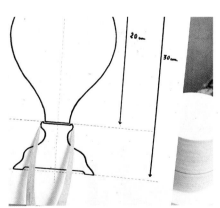

18
Now measure the height of the foot of the vase with the compasses.

19
Again show this size on the cylinder with the compasses and pencil.

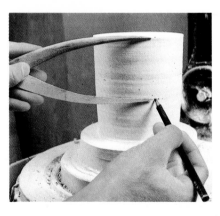

20
Measure the top of the foot where the main part of the vase goes.

21

Show this size on the top of the plaster cylinder with the compasses and then draw the circle with a pencil.

22

Slowly begin removing the plaster, following the lines of the diagram exactly.

23

Use a suitable cutting tool to make the hollow between the bottom and top part of the foot so that it is quite smooth.

24

Now make the bottom part of the foot, which has a sort of collar, as shown in the diagram.

25

Remove plaster from the surface at the top to make a hollow.

26

Use a sharp cutting tool to make a groove just below the foot. This indicates where the foot will be cut off from the base.

27

Make the groove deeper with a piece of nylon wire. Now the foot will easily come off.

28

The foot is ready. The main part of the vase should fit on this exactly.

29
The rest of the plaster cylinder is used to make the lid.

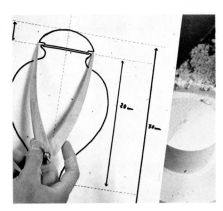

30
Transfer this size onto the cylinder and draw the circle onto the cylinder with a pencil.

31
Now measure the height of the lid with the compasses.

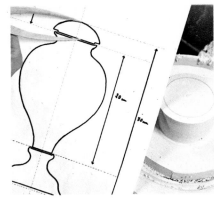

32
Again show this size on the side of the cylinder. The pencil circle indicates the bottom edge of the lid.

33
Using the diagram as a guide, give the lid its rounded shape.

34
When the profile of the lid is correct, make the bottom edge. It should fit exactly in the hollow at the top of the main part of the vase.

35
Cut into the plaster with the nylon wire so that the lid easily comes off.

36
The lid is now finished. It should fit exactly and the whole vase can be assembled.